Rafferty's Rules

BY

FRANK RAFFERTY

Salamander Street

First published in 2024 by Salamander Street Ltd.
(info@salamanderstreet.com)

A CIP catalogue record for this book is available from the British Library.

Cover illustration: 'Stone' by Rachael Johnson

ISBN: 9781738429363

10 9 8 7 6 5 4 3 2 1

Wordville

ACKNOWLEDGEMENTS

Marion & Frank, whose often operatic relationship taught me how to be and not to be in the world.

Rachael, for all of this love. which I often don't deserve.

Eoin, who infuriates me sometimes, makes me laugh often, cry occasionally, curse regularly and love unconditionally.

Mark Patterson and all his team at BBC Radio Foyle.

Family and friends, here and gone, whom I love and miss.

And to all the bastards met and yet to come. I know where you live, or I can make an educated guess and find you later.

ABOUT FRANK RAFFERTY

Frank Rafferty was born in the last days of the Ross Maternity Hospital, Paisley, which shortly afterwards was repurposed (what a vile word) as a psychiatric institution. Despite his protestations, many of his family and friends claim that this drastic change in usage was somehow connected to his arrival into the world.

Poetry may not have been in the blood but shortly after the birth, his Uncle Reg, who arrived in Glasgow from Kingston, Jamaica, via London and knew Gil Scott-Heron's Da, proclaimed at one of the many and regular extended, drunken, rowdy family gatherings that: "this boy has the brow of a poet."

Frank's mother, Marion, tried to drive this notion from his head from an early age, reasoning that there was no money in poetry and little likelihood of that changing. She also noticed that some of his attempts at spoken word and verse seemed to induce rage and violence towards him, by some of his peers and a few teachers had words with her about the scurrilous nature of his writings.

Any way, time passed and his addiction to words stayed with him, through education and his expulsion from it, a wide variety of low level jobs (Sales, Labouring, Bars/Clubs/Hotels, Fishmonger, Bus Conductor, etc.,) which along with his being in several bands, took him to many various towns and cities, the length and breadth of the UK (from Shetland to the Channel Islands). He eventually went back into education, attending Salford University and Wolverhampton Polytechnic, subsequently working in adult education, community development and the arts sector.

Frank now resides in Derry, in the north of Ireland working with an arts organisation in the Bogside area of the city (Gasyard Bluebell Arts). The title of the organisation reminds him, daily, for reasons best known to himself, of Alan Ginsberg's *Sunflower Sutra*. He claims that such small blessings, make even the administrative aspect of his work bearable.

Throughout his life, Frank has created poetry and been a performer, punk rock singer, occasional actor and stand-up comedian. Over the past two decades or so, he has returned to re-engaging with the craft of the spoken word artist. Frank is also the organiser of the All Ulster Poetry Slam Championship and co-organiser of the All Ireland Poetry Slam Championship and has been involved with the organisation and programming of events for several arts festivals in Northern Ireland including FLive, The Big Oak Literary Festival, Aspects Festival, Severe Burns (an alternative Burns Night) and several others.

He performs extensively as a spoken word artist and occasional comedian at various clubs, venues and arts, poetry and music festivals throughout the UK and Ireland.

He also features in an experimental punk band called *The Dead Thatchers*. Proceeds from sales of their work go to foodbanks in Glasgow.

Photo Credit: Éamonn Brown

FOREWORD/INTRODUCTION

I am aware that often the foreword to a book is written by someone else, sometimes a friend or colleague of the poet.

The reason for this book being called *Rafferty's Rules* is that the term is 20th Century Australian Slang meaning there are no rules at all.

Bearing that in mind, I'm writing my own foreword, or is it my own introduction? Call it what you wish. Chances are if you're reading this, you've bought this collection. If so, thank you. I hope you enjoy the experience.

There is no poem in this collection, or elsewhere titled *Rafferty's Rules*. I'm a spoken word poet and, although my work has been published in a variety of journals over the years, I've always been hesitant to commit my work to the page.

I am thankful that the wonderful publisher of this book was persuasive enough to convince me that a collection of my recent poetry would be a welcome addition to the world.

I'm also grateful to Mark Patterson and all his team at BBC Radio Foyle for giving me access to a much wider audience than most poets can ever dream of.

I hope that the work contained here will, in turns, move, amuse and engender thoughtful pauses in the reader. If anyone finds anything objectionable or offensive within these pages., it is never my intention to cause offence, it is just something that sometimes happens with me. I would apologise but being Glaswegian, I feel it is my duty to explain that the word sorry is just our shorthand for "excuse me", which may be intoned in various ways, with or without a question mark and in Glaswegian, only ever really means can you let me past you, or did I hear you right? I mention this in passing, as there are poems within which are written phonetically, in Glaswegian. I invite you to attempt to think in my accent, as you read them, which will certainly be educational for some of you.

Anyway, that's my foreword/introduction.

Cheerio.

Frank Rafferty
2024

P.S: It will also be possible to purchase recordings of some of the work contained in this collection by streaming content on Spotify, Bandcamp, Mixcloud etc., or purchasing a CD directly via tlufs59@gmail.com or at www.frankraffertyspokenwordpoet.com

The recordings are a mix of material found in this collection and other work, some with added music and soundscapes.

CONTENTS

ABSENT

hmmm, hmm, hm, hm, hmm, my darling.
The doom will be mine, if I stay

I write these words to tease my tongue,
Remembering then, when we were young
And brightest blades that danced through town.
Those upright days of no come down,
We thought the world just brass and muck,
But we had the gift, the looks, the luck
And never thought we could be cool, or old, or dead
And we were cruel, as young boys turning men can be.
We lived our impropriety.
Two glorious whirling dervish Dans,
    who bore no weapons in our hands,
Avoiding those more flat and dull, we favoured thought,
    our minds grew full
And fat on what was happening now.
We murdered every sacred cow,
Just to upset each bourgeois prig,
Was our joie de vivre.
Boy! We were sick.

'tis far better to part though it`s hard to
than rot in the prison away

Then time moves on and rivers flow.
You stayed behind. I had to go.
There was just so much to be had out there
    and our affectations grew thread bare,
Oh! Those drugs we never cleaned, or shared.
I went away,

1

We were both touched, by times we lived in but not so
  much
As others whom I'd seen grow mad, being squandered in
  the lives they had.
We knew that we would meet again and we'd converse
  like now was then,
When future days would bring us back to planning out
  some new attack
On all that someone else holds dear. I hadn't planned to
  disappear,
Completely, gone into life elsewhere. It's not as if I didn't care
But time grew scarcer with my work, with less time off to
  go berserk.
Then months, then years, we let things slip.
Then every new relationship
And hundreds and hundreds of miles away, we think
  we'll catch up soon.
Some day.

in a day I`ll be over the mountain,
there`ll be time enough left for to cry

A damp and dirty, semi-derelict room. A resting place, A
  scabby doom.
You huddled in that old raincoat. No letters left. No
  clear-cut note.
You simply scrawled out on the wall,
Don't find me. I'm not here, at all. Then spilled yourself.
I miss you, Paul.

so.. goodnight and god guard you forever
and write to me won`t you. Goodbye

NOTES FROM THE ASYLUM

"The whole religious complexion of the modern world is due to the absence from Jerusalem of a lunatic asylum." Thomas Paine

There is a list of the names of the dead,
Would you prefer silence? Their names left unsaid?
Gunned down by soldiers protected by states,
Who view protest as criminal.
This was the fate of all of those people
    now listed as dead.
Do you prefer silence? Their names left unsaid?

Men, women, children. Abandoned, dead, bleeding.
Because they protest? Do you think this misleading?

There can never be violence.
Unless by the state.
Whose murder is not murder?
Whose hate is not hate?

The lambs and the doves are killed, under the eagle.
And government spokespeople, tell us this was legal.
A sensible action, absolved from above.
For wolves hid among all the lambs and the doves.
You may not have seen them.
But we know they were there.
And our soldiers shot only at them. They were scared.

Bodies amass by the fence and the wall.
Some people are labelled not as people at all.
The state will use only proportionate force.
And the protesters, as always, were violent. Of course,

That explains everything that happened. It makes sense.
Our soldiers are always our last line of defence.
If you view events, differently, wherever you are?
Whether you live here or watch from afar,
Your mounting revulsion, sides you with all haters.
Your mounting revulsion, numbers you with the traitors.

For we too have lists of the names of our dead.
Their names and their killers will not be unsaid.
And although our list is smaller,
It carries more weight,
Than the lists of our enemies.
We are the state.

The soldier goes home, sleeps unsoundly in bed.
Here is a list of the names of the dead.

PAST LIVES

Remembering my past lives can be quite funny,
All those times, when I was them and never me,
I've never been an aristocrat or foreign doctor.
But there are many lives I've lived being a tree.
They'll always talk of channelling past lives, as a human.
Witches, bankers, criminals, kings and thieves
It's all accents, sex, demeanour, occupation.
They never talk about the bark, or nuts or leaves.

They never mention wildlife, rot, rodents or loud birds
    nesting.
They won't discuss that crazy woodsman with his axe,
Or being the prop from which they're found sometimes,
    just hanging.
You'll not find that outlined in the Past Lives Book Of
    Facts.
It's always fascinating adventures abroad as someone
Other than who you are. A Duchess or a Lord,
A criminal mastermind, a one-legged highway woman.
Or some dude who invented guns, or sharpened swords.

They won't even whisper of being felled, deep in the forest,
They don't talk of being chopped up to make a chair.
There's a lot more to most past lives than being a human.
Not that many, if any, of you shallow creatures care.

But at least when I was a tree, life was unhurried,
I was out there, in nature, firmly rooted, free.
What is the reason why such lives are lived unworried?
There is no I, nor mind to think with, being a tree.

That's why remembering all of my past lives can be quite
    funny.
When I talk of them, as if they're something being missed.
For all my past lives, tree or human, just like yours
were things imagined only. They never did exist.

I STOPPED

I stopped
When finally
The penny dropped

And I
Realised
That God
Was simply
Santa Claus
For Grown Ups

MICKEY'S MONKEY

Do you know? Snow can burn you
When standing too close
To the High Sheriff Mountain transmission mast
In a snow storm

Can burn you so bad you'd need skin grafts

An old pirate radio man told me that
One night
When we were drunk

No. Not the guy who had that show
On his illicit broadcasting station,

A show called Mickey's Monkey

After that song that's played on the car radio,
Aaah! Harvey Keitel
As De Niro dances in the headlights

And you just know De Niro will die,
Even though there's so much love there,
Up on that screen,
In those moments,
Passing between them like sound waves.

Aye, so
Never go near the High Sheriff Mountain transmission mast
With devices to boost your auld signal,
In a snow storm.

Snow can burn you,
So bad
You'd need skin grafts.

So painful
It might even hurt more than love.

YOUR HEALTH

For our NHS

My grandparents could barely breathe from tightening
   their belts,
Is it hard now to imagine all the terror which they felt?
Each time when they or one of theirs was sick or taken ill,
Could they afford the medicine? A £2 doctor's bill?
Yet each and every time today, our families are unwell.
Health care is free, for her, for me. Now there's a tale to tell!
You grant me that serenity which they had never known,
From their collective will you sprang, completely ours,
   home grown.

My Dad's sister Patricia, she was the aunt I'd never meet,
Back then pneumonia often brought a funeral to the street.
But no magic spell did summon you, you are our own creation.
You were demanded... and out you came... from post war
   devastation.
You embody love for everyone and still we understate
Your true value and your worth to us, since 1948.
You grant me the serenity that those before me had not
   known.
From their collective will you sprang, completely ours, home
   grown.

If and when we can, we pay so that if and when there's need;
By her, by me, by neighbours, strangers, friends. You'll
    intercede,
With doctors, nurses, hospitals, new treatments for our pain.
You act as salve and balm when we are wounded or insane.
We'll never know, because of you, the fear people once felt.
Poor people who could barely breathe from tightening their
    belts.
You grant me the serenity which they had never known
From their collective will you sprang, completely ours,
    home grown.

Your Health was first published in *Celine's Salon - The Anthology Volume 2*.

ELEPHANT

Everyone
Ignored
The Elephant
In the room.

Even after,
I had climbed up,
Onto his back,
Sat in the Howdah
And began to smash
The furniture
Into pieces.

ARAPHEL

A Hebrew word, Araphel can mean darkness where light waits or is hidden.

The brutality of your strength advances terror,
Responding to each error of your mind,
You cannot keep land still also home to others.
This is that deeper truth you must yet find.

Land. Once home to ancient ancestors who wondered,
If those who'd made them leave would ever make amends,
While other lives, for four millenia, had wandered,
Along these shores. Planted olive trees.
Women and men,

Who, when you returned, they helped you carry water,
They helped you to build, were glad to co-exist,
Yet among you, some planned on driving out and slaughter
Of such welcomes, on the basis of a myth.
Some ancient fable of the mind has gave them power.
Convincing lies can only ever spread,
Advancing out through notions of blood, of soil, of nation,
Advancing over other bodies and their dead

This lust for land, for place, for home, often distorted
To be seen as high above, all those already there.
Crushes all of our good natures. This desire
Stamps down the love that teaches all to share.
Brutality through strength advances terror,
Increased by each sad lie you now design,
With tank, warplane, shell and bullet, as children cower,
Around the world. People stand up, for Palestine.

TEMPLEMORE

For the peace, written on the morning of day 666 of no NI Assembly—the last time.

Not pretending to understand. No idea at all.
Some years ago on an election night.
They came in and they cleared out the hall.

Outside folk stood chatting and smoking,
I thought you were taking the hand
you said: "There might be a bomb in the car park."
I said: "What The Fuck?" Then I ran,
when I realised that you weren't joking.
I jogged on, off over that field.
The rest of you stood there, laughing and smoking.
I couldn't believe this was real.

How could that ever seem normal?
I ran. Aye I did. And so what?
My heart was just battering my chest out,
My stomach was an aching, tight knot.

Back home I went into his bedroom
I sat there, just breathing my fear.
His head fast asleep, on the pillow.
Why has this all happened here?

As I sat there, so quiet, in that darkness,
A gulp down deep into my throat
I thought of that story you told me
Of the wee boy who died on that boat.

A boy just enjoying the summer,
At work, never thinking he'd die

And the 2 of you waving down, from the headland,
Under a blazing blue sky.
All that wreckage, all those hearts torn asunder
All those people, all those lives, your poor friend
All that madness, all that utter destruction.
Yet somehow you've made it all, nearly end.

Later, I'm still sat there. Not sleeping.
Then a sound, from the distance, from the dark
Kind of a WHUUUMPF! An explosion?
You only wake up when the dogs starts to bark.

Templemore was first published in *Celine's Salon - The Anthology Volume 2*.

MEN WHO CAN'T STOP MARCHING

Here are some men who can't stop marching, bowler hats
    pressed down on ears.
Each July, in every village and every town down all the
    years,
See the banners waving boldly, see the sashes proudly wore,
In Rasharkin, in Desertmartin. Here are the men who
    know the score.

Here's to those men who shan't stop marching, who see
    no evil as they walk,
Will hear no evil of their neighbours, even those of
    different stock,
As they commemorate old battles from some long
    forgotten war,
They know still why they are marching and what those
    battles were fought for.

In Rossnowlagh , Derry, Fivemiletown, Larne,
    Cullybackey too.
Are Men who'll not stop marching, marching somewhere
    close to you?
On these parades I see far fewer younger people every
    year.
And on the faces of those marching seems a sadness or
    a fear.

We are the men who won't stop marching, followed by
    our winning votes.
With our pipes and flutes still distant, you will hear our
    plaintive notes.

And the thunder of our banging sticks on stretched out
  skins of goats,
Which may attract some knuckle draggers, trailing
  tattered, mucky coats.

We are those men born to a culture in a time we did
  not pick,
The under siege men and their brethren, whom your
  conscience will not prick.
We were born to serve this purpose until we meet the
  dead and quick.
And just to serve as a distraction, Let's watch the monkey
  throw his stick.*

(half sung, half spoken)
Here we come
Walking down your street
We get the funniest looks
From everybody we meet
Hey! Hey!

* 'stick monkey' is a Glaswegian term used to describe the guy
  leading such parades.

SNAKE

Inspired by a conversation between two young women on a bus.

"Where'd you get tae last night?"   "Efter the party?"
"Aye"   "I went aff wi' yer man"
"Did you stay wi' him? Aw night?"   "Aye"
"Ach! Ye need tae mind yirself. Ye know whit they're like"
                              "Aye but this wiz different"
"Whit dae ye mean?"   "He said that me he loved me"
"But they aw say that."
                    "Aye. But he said he loved me so much that,
                        if he could, he'd move intae my skin."

MMAJIN

"Art is anything which pushes our thoughts in important yet neglected directions" - Alain De Botton

Mmajin
Thi horrur ae thi hoor
Hoo gaun doon
Oan a pyoor mingin puntir
Jist fur a seckind
Ackshilly sterts tae enjoay it
Jist fur a seckind
Mmajin
N then ask mi
How ah feel aboot ma wurk

MY GRANNY MADE ME AN ANARCHIST

For Stuart Christie

My Granny made me an anarchist
That night when she came up with my bail
She said: "Frankie, son, always box clever
Never let them put you into a jail"
Never let them know what you're thinking,
Nor let them know that you intend their demise,
If they stop you in the street, just keep smiling.
And remember
A smile always starts in your eyes.

Read a lot, Have many friends, enjoy talking,
Have a beer or three but never to excess
Experiment with whatever you want to
But keep in mind, more is rarely better than less
Have sex with whoever you want to,
Who takes your fancy or you to their bed
But try never to break any promises made
And Keep religion well away from your head

She was just a wee wumman fae Springburn
Who claimed that she didnae know very much
But when she went into the intricacies of anarcho-syndicalist
    thought
At first I thought she was speaking in Dutch
She said there is a coming insurrection
You may not know when or where but the why
Is all that we can ever be sure of
That and the fact that we'll die

There's this world and there won't be another
We'll no be building new homes in the stars
That's Science Fiction? Keep the emphasis on fiction!
And politicians will leave you nothing but scars
They'll try to Dupe you, lie to you
Don't believe them
Or their facts of the matter. It's all lies.
No matter which party they claim to stand for
They're all the same wan, with some in disguise.

Now Granny never danced with Emma Goldman
Didny drink with Bakunin, Rudi Rocker or Emma Par-
    sons
But she taught me that revolt is a natural tendency of life
And that a case may be well made for arson
Direct Action said my Granny is necessity
The world can be whatever all of us create
Beyond decrees and control of parties and leaders
And there can be no redress from the state
Government isn't there for the governed
But serves the interests of the rulers and the rich
The rest of us are merely a game to be played
By those who'll never die in any ditch.

Aye, My Granny made me an anarchist
That night when she came up with my bail
She said: " Frankie, son, always box clever
Never let them put you into their jail."

My Granny Made Me An Anarchist was first published in *Celine's Salon - The Anthology Volume 2.*

JAZZ

Jag eyed, walkin' to music,
Wildly wailin' & wow!
Electric spark, soul limbo shuffle,
A tellin' of where to & how.
Stumblin' down alley-run music, hard-eyed & howlingly
wailed,
Bejewelled & yet frantically ruffled, over tomorrow it
sailed,
On, on, on into horizons, bending, rending & yow!
Heart spotted, then blown into never
To tumble us back into now.

SERVICE 64

The Service 64 bus runs from Derry to Galway, via Letterkenny & many other stops.

My shirt spoke in Egyptian, my mind dissolved away to dust,
My hands turned almost transparent, my motor skills
    were very sus.
I saw through superficiality and beneath our planet's crust,
Your head moved very slowly, I didn't make a fuss.
That was the night I swallowed acid on the
    Letterkenny Bus.

There was laughter, there were colours, which were
    pulsing, there were many.
You didn't have a coat on, I kept thinking who killed Kenny,
Patterns danced across a tablecloth, a sound of Vidi Vici
    Veni.
I was high as that French pole vaulter, Renaud Lavillenne.
That night I dropped some acid on the bus to
    Letterkenny.

I was Raftery the poet, if Raftery had lost his mind.
I had my seventh vision while I thought am I going blind?
You were sheltering a hidden key, which none of us could
    find.
Meanwhile clouds, planets, stars everything aligned.
On a bus a man (who's me?) seeks for the
    Letterkenny sign.

Neil deGrasse Tyson talks of universes made of light,
While ours is dark but matters only when we truly catch a
    sight,
Of our own grotesque potential to make everything a fight,
Or reduce our deepest thoughts into a media-bled soundbite.
Meanwhile... on the Letterkenny Bus, there sits a wide-eyed
    sybarite.

I was happy as a sandboy but I don't know what sandboys are.
Do they talk to friendly sailors? Do they like to have a jar?
Do they just exist in Ireland, are they known
        both wide and far?
Does it matter? I was happy, maybe even happier
        than they are.
It's easy tripping on a bus somewhere but never drive your car.

Later. Later? There were patterns all swirling on the walls,
when I went into the toilet, they were swarming in the hall,
On your hands, your face, your body,
        they're there too but very small.
How would I feel if I had just been drinking alcohol?
Would the bus have got here quicker if I'd taken bugger all?

What's that music? Do I know it? I think I've known it well.
Somewhere in my past, it was a sound that would foretell,
That in this exact momentum, we'd be standing here, as well.
Time and space cannot be linear. Is someone singing
        Rebel Yell?
There's a guy sporting a Mohawk, is he on
        this acid bus as well?

Once there was a merry prankster, Acid Eric was his name.
He drove a bus through India. Years beyond? Before?
    The fame
Of travelling, with Kesey and Neal Cassady, plugged into
    that mainframe
Of early psychotropic travellers, both the brilliant
    and the lame.
Did Timothy Leary ever wait, for a bus that never came?

Am I still in Derry, stationary? This could be any place.
My thoughts all seem as fragile as the bones
    behind my face.
Am I a screen you've put words into, a command line
    interface?
This seems like paranoia now, yet still a state of grace.
This bus is a small craft, now lost in interstellar space.

Yet I'm sat on a floor beside you now. I know and realise
That I'm a laughing sack of skin. Then we start to
    harmonise.
We both go out there, past the byways of
    wherever reason lies.
The night is dark and so much older than whatever
    money buys.
I see through this Letterkenny bus, I've no needs left to
    analyse.

The state we're in is inconsistent
Moved by much more than love and lust.
All of this may dematerialize, we might need to readjust.
All of our grand expectations. We are but white pine
    blister rust.

We remain confounded by each other, seeds deep sown by
    lack of trust.
Then suddenly, there is time, again: "Is this the Derry bus?
Was my journey long? O my weary bones,
Feels as if I've swam the Shannon.
My mouth and brain have been fried, then disco-stomped
    a la Bohannon, Bohannon, Bohannon,
If my body was a temple, they would need to get a man in
To carry out urgent repairs. Then add me to that canon
Of wans on buses, who've sat a long time chatting with
    Tuatha De Danann*

---

* originally children, tribe or people of the goddess Danu. Eventually
    meaning the faeries.

BEING A TREE

I stood, in the centre of the living room. Just being a tree.
I had first been a tree, aged 8 years old.
Springburn co-operative hall. My 7 year old neighbour
Sang the Skye Boat song, sweetly.
I was a tree,
Humiliated, bile rising and with a strong thirst for
    vengeance,
I was a tree.

12 months later, during a game of rounders,
On our street, accidentally, on purpose,
With one careless swing of the bat,
The, by then, 8 year old wicket keeper,
Caught my vengeance full, with his face.
Why there was a wicket keeper during our game of
    rounders,
Was entirely due to my powers of persuasion.
Why, some 50 odd years later, I am still just being a tree
Is quite frankly baffling, particularly for the neighbours,
Who peer through my window, from the street.

DO NOT BELONG TO OTHERS

Do not belong to others for none belong to you,
possession is—not virtue—just the turning of a screw.
All those dispossessed possessions, spent and broken on the
    rack,
Do not belong to others for they may not give you back.

It really doesn't matter if it's me, you, her or him,
Who can become someone's possession, be disposed of,
    on a whim.
A darker-still scenario for her, him, me or you,is to become
    someone's possessor.
Do I belong to you?

Do I belong to you now? Do you belong to me?
Is this all that I long for? To give someone the key
To understand me, totally (accept without complaint),
To give to this one other, my whole self, without restraint?
Abandoned to that moment when another makes me live,
When against all wiser judgement I can do naught else but
    give
All my love (head, heart and body)
To this single other soul,
To unite in the divisions of our selves and make us whole.
Still the Siren voices call, hear their claims,
    ask "are they true?:
"Do not belong to others for none belong to you."
"Do not be led by instinct, love, emotion you can feel."
"Kneel before each endless reason for denying what is real."

"Break the heart"   "Destroy the spirit"
"Kill all passion"   "Murder rage"
"Purge your memory of loving"   "Build yourself a better cage"
"Try to wriggle out of living"   "Climb the scaffold"
                     "Bend the knee"
"Do not belong to others they may never set you free"

Free to feel no thing for no one.
Free to gasp the truth of Zen.
Free to mutter through the madness in the minds of
    many men:
How you're free of fruitless passion,
How you're crucified inside,
How your science, your gods, your reason have all being
    verified.
I don't want such understanding. I don't need to live
    alone
I know we all are anyhow from belly back to bone.
I just need your heartfelt laughter. I want your body next
    to mine.
Belonging to another is the only human sign.

Back to this. That same old story, told and telling, always true.
I may not belong to others
but I will belong to you.

THIS IZ THI VOYS

Responding to a theory that the working classes have a 'restricted codes' of communication

This iz thi voys
Ma ain Itwiz loast
Bit sumhow Ah keptit
Nae mattir thicost
Itwiz loast Ah hid birrydit
Unner mountains ashite
N then Ahwint aff sumwherr
N tried speaking right
Birrit jist didny sootmi
It leftmi tungtied
Ach! Ah wiz left feelin lowzi
Like sumbiddyd died
Inmaheed ahwiz hurtin, Sumhin jist wizni clickin
Ma langwij Ma cultshir
Hidbin geein agood kickin
Izawain itaw startid
Wicomix n books
N iffah askdah kwestjin
Ahdgit wannae thurlooks
Thit sayd Ah wizrubbish
Ah cheynjd how ahspoak
Tullaw ae mateechurs
Thoat ah wiznae ajoak
Ciz Scots wiraw styoopit
Drunk Mental Vylint
Glasweejinz wurwurs

I spoke and grew silent.

I grew silent and weary,
I felt a deep sense of shame.
I spoke with my new voice
And then, I came
Hame

Ah stoapt n ah lissind fur thifurst time inyeerz
Ah stull hidan axent
Thit moovdmi tae teerz
Ah stoapt n ah liissind withoot beein priperrd
Ah lissind tae peepul
N ah likedwhit ahherd
Ah stoapt beein frightened a beein gramatikly wrang
Nah spoak in ma ain voys
Naw ah didni...   Aah... SANG

NAE PASARAN YA BASS[1]

Here are the people who never ran,
Who'll stand and fight for everywan,
People that polis should rightly fear,
Refugees are welcome here.
Let Glasgow Flourish.

Where people are full of funny stories,
Where people will truly fuck the Tories,
Where people know for who we fight
And wullnae believe your racist shite
Let Glasgow Flourish.

Don't sneak back at night, we'll still be there,
This is still a place where people care.
A place where people still like their neighbours
And help them wi' their daily labour
Let Glasgow Flourish.

Where we march to the beat o' a different drum,
This city that knows our day will come,
Let Glasgow Flourish.
Where strangers are pals we've no met yet
Where auld wimmin'll ask: Are ye awright, pet?
Let Glasgow Flourish.

Let a thousand Kenmure Streets[2] now bloom.
You're welcome here, there's plenty of room.
Let Glasgow Flourish

We'll no be the first. We'll no be the last
To say: Nae Pasaran Ya Bass[3].
Let Glasgow Flourish.
Aye.
We'll no be the first, we'll no be the last
To say: Nae Pasaran Ya Bass.
Let Glasgow Flourish.

1 No Pasaran was a slogan of those who fought fascism in the
   Spanish Civil War.
2 Kenmure Street: where Glaswegians prevented Home Office vans
   deporting their asylum-seeking neighbours,
3 Ya Bass some claim is derived from a Gaelic warcry. In 1960s
   Glasgow it often followed gang names on walls.

A RANDOM SELECTION FROM 100 THINGS THAT KEEP ME AWAKE AT NIGHT

33. My fear of the hipsters with their strange votive offerings; their artworks made entirely of canvas (unpainted, of course) and their price on everything, sentient or otherwise, within that strange boutique in Hoxton.

49. The possible existence of starched pyjamas.

10. Worrying about if I'm breathing, incorrectly.

72. A sad memory of bagpipe music.

26. Accusations of sock puppetry by the invisible guardians of undeserved reputation on Wikipedia.

27. Why is there only one a in Wikipedia?

32. Mental images of Hel (with only one L) which is real and is an actual town in Norway.

39. Birds of prey—more specifically, an eagle. A perfectly understandable fear, born of reading too much Greek mythology (without appropriate adult supervision) at the tender age of 6, or maybe 7, and realising the limitations of my own non-regenerative liver.

40. My non-regenerative liver and the punishment which I have more recently and regularly subjected this flaw to. (DRINK).

69. Roko's Basilisk—No! Don't Google it, don't even think about it. I'm sorry. Too late.

5. The inert gases and their place in the periodic table.

6. My fear that every song ever written about the periodic table is quickly out of date.

57. The dawning of the age of Aquarius and how disappointed all of the non-Aquarians might be.

58. My irrational fear that the non-Aquarian sense of disappointment will be stirred up by demagogues and boil over into some sort of mass persecution of Aquarians, of which I am one.

94. Imagining deformed melting models of Christ and Mohammad made entirely from Gorgonzola cheese.

47. Love and all of the people who lack it.

18. Questions such as: "Do porn stars really have private parts?"

12. My inner child and the faecal matter which he intends to make me eat, in the future.

28. My dread of public sleep masturbation.

13. Your inner child and all that she may come to represent, in the future.

66. A song called the Tennessee Waltz.

84. Horrific imagery on cigarette packets, warning me of damage to my optic nerves, which I cannot see properly because smoking has damaged my optic nerves.

14. All of your inner children, in the future.

75. Thinking about this reality being a parallel universe and how did I get here.

92. (*plays harmonium*) My complete lack of musical ability and my persistent yet futile ownership of several musical instruments.

76. The end of the universe as I have finally stopped worrying about its beginning.

15. The inspectors from inner children in need, who will eventually call round to inspect everybody's houses, in the future.

7. Your knees.

27. Thoughts of Nirvana, both the theological concept and Kurt Cobain's band.

8. My knees.

42. My sense of apprehension that barely half-remembered nightmares from my childhood will return to claim me, tonight.

9. The knees of the total stranger, who may or may not have been a psychopath but we killed anyway, disposing of the entire body, apart from the bony bleached knee bones, which we kept as souvenirs and occasionally use as weird sex toys.

98. Fragments from partial conversations overheard on buses, 17 years ago.

2. The phrase "Be still, my beating heart." I mean, really, why would anyone ever say that?

20. An instruction manual for killing things, which I found, one day, on a 64 bus going to Galway.

23. The tear-in-the-soul voice of Maighread Ni Ghrasta.

35. Fizzy water, Hiawatha, dripping snotter and other equally excruciating rhymes.

50. Imaginary gangs of marauding monkeys with hammers.

48. The fact that blue is not the warmest colour and the knowledge that if I state such facts aloud, there are actually people in this world who will somehow view such a statement as criticism of the entire premise of the film *Blue Is The Warmest Colour*... which I have not even seen.

55. My complicity in the mass murder of animals, simply so that I can grow ever more obese and the ensuing justified judgements being passed on me, by acolytes of the philosopher Peter Singer and others.

63. (*yawn*) Counting sheep and wondering what are they counting and when did they open that special sheep school to teach the little woolen fuckers to count anyway. Goddamit! I may as well just get up again now.

1. That last lost wild look in the eyes of my long gone, gone, gone, Daddy. Oh!

WHEN I DIE

Will I wade in the tide of your memories?
Decline on the shores of your dream?
From there become a few dots in your painting?
Or be photoshopped into a meme?
A trace of me found in an old jacket pocket
May keep you awake in your bed.
Odd thoughts of me fading from view on a ghat
May remain with you
When I am dead.
Happy Times, beer, bread and laughter.
There was love, there was some tenderness,
There was sex, then more laughter and a sense of ourselves.
There never was really much less.
But death?
That's the last thing anyone thinks may happen
When you're simply here, taking in air
Your breathing seems strong, your pulse isn't shallow
Then Bam! and...
You're no longer there.
May I waken old lovers, at night, into tears
May I still make a friend laugh in thought
Of a memory of me, in my pomp, then laugh harder
Sure, that's about the sum of our lot.
As the ash blows away and the wind swirls around
And forests lang linger and dree
When the night is quite still,
Bar the thrum of the rain
On the roof of a room which housed me.
I never thought this could be possible
To think of me not being there

To not see strong feeling ablaze in your eyes
To not bury my face in your hair.
Was there just nothing left here to hold onto,
I floated off into my dream,
Where it seems I fell into the silence, the darkness
No light, not a spark, not a gleam.
Deep into this essence of darkness.
Can you still recall how I smell?
When all have gone who may have once said my name.
Is that truly the Final Farewell?
Where the rocks meet the sand
Kiss the water
Stick a note in a bottle from me
Ask your deity to let me go gentle
Then fling the bottle far out, for the sea.

REMAINDER

and everything away again... except the trace within...

a salty tang, then sweet as blood,

your taste of singing skin

and everything away again... stilled memories collect...

the smell of you,

a smile, a hair,

on such 'is'ness I reflect,

then, quite unwilled,

a tear appears... without regret or pain...

in bed I lay one day with you,

then all is gone again...

the skin between your shoulder blades,

my hand between your thighs,

your arms, your hair, your breasts, your breath, your
mouth, your cunt, your eyes.

I taste you still, I feel your heat, I kissed you and remain
within your mind—remember me...

when all is gone again.

LASTWURDS

How kin a wurd coz sich oafens?
Dae they hink thurz bitza langwij
Shid bi left oot, unimploayd?
Shid ah avoayd whit bitz agreev thur petty sens a bein'?
Shid aw thit tokit diffrintly
jist sit oan thi fens
N let thaim disyd whit ivryhin shid meen?
N lissin bit no tok attaw,
jist grunt?
Heer whit ahm sayin' noo?
Ah bet yi dae. Ya cunt!

ALSO AVAILABLE FROM SALAMANDER STREET

All Salamander Street plays can be bought in bulk at a discount for performance or study. Contact info@salamanderstreet.com to enquire about performance licenses.

CELINE'S SALON VOLUME 1

ISBN: 9781838403638

An anthology of work by 29 writers, songwriters and artists who have performed at Soho's literary cabaret Celine's Salon.

CELINE'S SALON VOLUME 2

ISBN: 9781739103026

Poetry, short-stories and song lyrics from 29 contributors to Celine's Salon.

JUAN BY JUAN by Juan Ramirez, Jr.

ISBN: 9781914228971

A collection that explores life, identity and love by Puerto Rican and Guatemalteco, Bronx born and raised, Juan Ramirez, Jr.

HOPE IS A SILHOUETTE by Lana Mcdonagh

ISBN: 9781739103019

A body of intimate and introspective poetry with accompanying illustrations, both written and painted by Lana McDonagh.

MINERVA AND THE WHIR by Jo D'arc

ISBN: 9781838403614

Jo D'arc's magical text takes the reader on a journey across the elements as Minerva wakes and explores the earth.

i am ill with hope by Gommie

ISBN: 9781914228575

Gommie's journey through poems and illustrations, offering bitesize snapshots of hope.